Celebrating Cultures

Oktoberfest

Jill Foran

WEIGL PUBLISHERS INC.

Published by Weigl Publishers Inc.
123 South Broad Street, Box 227
Mankato, MN, 56002, USA
Web site: www.weigl.com

Library of Congress Cataloging-in-Publication Data

Foran, Jill.
  Oktoberfest / by Jill Foran.
      p. cm. -- (Celebrating cultures)
Includes index.
Summary: Describes the history and various activities of Oktoberfest, a
festival that originated in Germany.
  ISBN 1-59036-094-X (lib. bdg. : alk. paper)
  1. Oktoberfest--United States--Juvenile literature. 2.
Oktoberfest--Juvenile literature. [1. Oktoberfest. 2. Festivals.] I.
Title.
  GT4403 .F66 2002
  394.2644--dc21

                           2002014571

Printed in the United States of America
1 2 3 4 5 6 7 8 9 0 06 05 04 03 02

Project Coordinator Heather Kissock **Design & Layout** Bryan Pezzi
Substantive Editor Christa Bedry **Photo Researcher** Wendy Cosh

Photograph Credits

Every reasonable effort has been made to trace ownership and to obtain permission to reprint copyright material. The publishers would be pleased to have any errors or omissions brought to their attention so that they may be corrected in subsequent printings.

Cover: German girl (Getty Images/C. Coleman); **Canadian Pacific Railway Archives Image No. NS 8454:** page 9T; **COMSTOCK Inc.:** page 9B; **Corbis Corporation:** pages 4 (Gunter Marx Photography), 7T, 14 (Adam Woolfitt); **Corel Corporation:** page 12B; **Eyewire Inc.:** pages 11T, 22; **Getty Images:** pages 6 (Sterflinger),8 (J. Hardtke), 10 (S. Studd); **Courtesy of Greater Cincinnati Convention & Visitors Bureau:** page 13MR; **Courtesy of Kitchener-Waterloo Oktoberfest:** pages 5, 11R, 15R; **Gary Marx:** pages 13BR, 15L; **MaXx Images:** pages 18; **Bryan Pezzi:** page 19T; **PhotoSpin Inc.:** pages 3, 12T; **Courtesy of RAM Productions Inc.:** page 13TR; **Monique de St. Croix:** page 19; **Courtesy of Travel Michigan:** page 11L; **Courtesy of Tulsa's Oktoberfest:** pages 7B, 13TL, 16, 17T, 17B, 21.

Contents

A German Celebration

Oktoberfest is a festival that celebrates German culture.

Millions of people all around the world look forward to Oktoberfest. This festival celebrates German culture. German Americans hold various Oktoberfest events across the United States. German Americans honor their **heritage** through these events. They also share their traditions with others. People from many different **ethnic groups** enjoy German music, food, and dancing during Oktoberfest.

People gather in the streets to celebrate Oktoberfest.

Oktoberfest is usually celebrated in September or October. The celebrations vary in length. Oktoberfest can last for weeks in some cities and towns. In other places, it lasts only a day. No matter how long, Oktoberfest celebrations are always a great deal of fun.

German Americans make up the largest ethnic group in the United States.

Oktoberfest is a time to renew old friendships and meet new people.

A Royal Event

The prince invited everyone to his wedding.

Oktoberfest began long ago in a city called Munich. Munich is the capital of Bavaria, which is a state in Germany. Prince Ludwig of Bavaria married Princess Therese on October 12, 1810. The prince wanted the residents of Munich to be present at his wedding. He invited all the people of Bavaria to attend his wedding.

Munich is located in the southeastern part of Germany.

Prince Ludwig's wedding was a grand occasion. More than 40,000 people came to the celebration. The guests enjoyed horse races, live music, and plenty of food. The party was such a success that Prince Ludwig decided to hold another party the following year. Oktoberfest soon became an **annual** event.

Many farmers **harvest** their crops in October. For this reason, Oktoberfest has also become harvest a celebration.

German bands entertain people at Oktoberfest celebrations.

Spreading the Cheer

Munich's Oktoberfest now includes carnival rides and a parade.

Munich's Oktoberfest became more popular as the years passed. By 1818, carnival rides were set up for the annual festival. A parade was added soon after. Traditional foods and drinks were served in huge tents. The day of fun and food soon turned into a celebration lasting 16 days. Every year, people from all across Germany look forward to Oktoberfest.

Munich's Oktoberfest is the largest public festival in the world.

Many German people **immigrated** to the United States during the 1800s and 1900s. They continued to honor their traditions in their new home. The first Oktoberfest celebrations in America were held in the late 1940s. These celebrations helped the German people honor their culture and homeland.

After World War II, German Americans held Oktoberfest celebrations in the United States to build friendly images of Germany.

Many families moved to the United States to build a new life.

Ellis Island was the arrival point for many European immigrants in the 1800s.

Oktoberfests Today

Special parades open Oktoberfest.

Today, hundreds of Oktoberfest celebrations are held across the United States. Crowds of people gather to celebrate German culture. Special parades often open the event. The parades feature marching bands and people dressed in traditional German clothing.

Lively marching bands add to the celebration of Oktoberfest.

A big party often follows the parade. The party features live music, dancing, and German foods. There are also plenty of activities for children. People of all ages take part in events, such as barrel races and **yodeling** contests.

Every year, more than 6 million people attend Munich's 16-day celebration. It is the largest Oktoberfest in the world.

Tubas are played throughout the Oktoberfest celebrations.

People of all ages enjoy the fun of Oktoberfest.

Americans Celebrate

Cities and towns all across the United States hold Oktoberfest celebrations each year. The largest Oktoberfests attract several thousands of people. Have a look at where some of the most popular Oktoberfests take place.

Seattle, Washington, hosts an Oktoberfest that lasts 2 days. Among the events are pumpkin-carving contests for children and adults.

One of the longest Oktoberfests is held in Torrance, California. It lasts from early September to the end of October. This Oktoberfest holds such fun events as pretzel-eating contests.

Seattle

Torrance

Fredericksb

About 200,000 people attend Oktoberfest in Tulsa, Oklahoma. They celebrate German traditions by eating delicious German foods and dancing the **polka**.

In Frankenmuth, Michigan, German Americans celebrate Oktoberfest every September.

Cincinnati, Ohio, hosts the largest Oktoberfest in the country. It is called Oktoberfest-Zinzinnati. Every September, more than 500,000 people attend the 2-day event.

Frankenmuth

Cincinnati

Isa

0   250   500 miles

The residents of Fredericksburg, Texas, celebrate Oktoberfest with live music, dance contests, and art shows.

Song and Dance

Oompah
music is lively
and catchy.

Oompah Music

German oompah music can be heard at every
Oktoberfest celebration. Traditional oompah music
is lively and energetic. It contains repetitive beats
and rhythms. Marching bands and other musical
groups perform this catchy music on stages across
the country. Oompah musicians play accordions,
clarinets, and brass instruments, such as tubas
and trombones.

Oompah bands play energetic music to
help keep people dancing.

Traditional Steps

Dancing is an important part of any Oktoberfest celebration. Crowds of people gather to watch as German folk dancers perform on stages. These dancers step to the music of the oompah bands. They perform graceful **waltzes** and lively polkas. One of the most popular folk dances is called the Schuplattler. It is a traditional Bavarian dance. The word "schuplattler" means "slapping the soles of shoes."

The Schuplattler was created in the 1600s by men who cut wood in the mountains. These men jumped around and slapped their legs to keep warm on cold nights.

Some German dances need only two people.

Other German dances require a group of people.

Dressing Up and Doing the Chicken

Dancers at Oktoberfest wear traditional German clothing.

Leather Shorts and Party Dresses

German dancers at Oktoberfest usually wear traditional clothing called *trachten*. Women and girls wear pretty dresses that are called *dirndls*. A dirndl has a close-fitting **bodice** and a full skirt. The men and boys wear leather shorts that are called *lederhosen*. Lederhosen are held up with suspenders. Sometimes the suspenders are decorated using a needle and colorful thread.

Wearing traditional clothing helps to preserve German culture.

Dancing Like a Bird

Everyone loves to do the Chicken Dance during Oktoberfest. In the 1950s, a Swiss man named Werner Thomas wrote a song to play on his accordion. Soon after, a dance was created for his song. The dance was called the Chicken Dance. Today, the Chicken Dance is a favorite event at Oktoberfests.

The largest Chicken Dance in the world took place in 1994 at Oktoberfest-Zinzinnati. More than 48,000 people did the Chicken Dance at the same time.

One part of the Chicken Dance requires the dancers to flap their arms like chickens.

Eat, Drink, and Be Merry

Food booths are set up all over the festival grounds.

Bratwursts and Pretzels

People love to feast on German foods during Oktoberfest. Food booths are set up all over the festival grounds. The booths serve all kinds of traditional German dishes. Hungry people can enjoy roasted chicken, many cheeses, sauerkraut, and a variety of sausages. One of the most popular German sausages is called bratwurst. It is made with pork and plenty of spices. Freshly baked pretzels are another favorite Oktoberfest treat.

Sauerkraut is pickled cabbage. It is normally served with sausages.

Sturdy Steins

At Oktoberfest, drinks are often served in special jugs that are called steins. A stein is a sturdy container that has a handle and a **hinged** lid. Steins are often decorated with images of colorful places and people. Some steins have scenes from history on them. Other steins have family **emblems** painted on their surface.

Oktoberfest drinks are also served in mugs. A mug has a handle, but does not have a lid.

Many people collect steins and display them in their homes.

For More Information

Many books and Web sites help explain the history and traditions of Oktoberfest. To learn more about Oktoberfest and German culture, you can borrow books from a library or research the Internet.

Books

Read the following books to learn more about Germany and its people.

Davis, Kevin A. *Look What Came from Germany*. London: Franklin Watts, 2000.

Lane, Kathryn. *Germany–the Culture*. New York: Crabtree Publishing Company, 2001.

Web Sites

For information on the largest Oktoberfest in the United States, visit **Oktoberfest-Zinzinnati** at: www.oktoberfest-zinzinnati.com

To see how the Chicken Dance is done, visit **Do the Chicken Dance** at: www.funpages.com/chickendance.htm

Enter the search word "Oktoberfest" into an online encyclopedia, such as **Encarta**. www.encarta.com

Imagine if...

Oktoberfest celebrations are held in many parts of the United States. While each celebration is a little different, they all honor German culture. Imagine that you and your friends must organize an Oktoberfest celebration. What events would you feature at your party? Would you have an oompah band? What kinds of German food would you serve? Would there be stages for dancing? Make a list of all the events you would feature at your own Oktoberfest. Then, draw a picture or write a report about the celebration.

What You Have Learned

1 Oktoberfest originated in Munich, Germany.

2 The first Oktoberfest celebrated the marriage of Prince Ludwig of Bavaria and Princess Therese.

3 Cities and towns throughout the United States hold Oktoberfest events to celebrate German culture.

4 The largest Oktoberfest in the United States takes place in Cincinnati, Ohio.

5 Pretzels and bratwursts are popular German foods.

6 German folk music and dancing are always a part of Oktoberfest.

More Facts to Know

- Munich's Oktoberfest takes place on a field called *Theresienwiese*. This is the German word for "Therese's fields."

- In Munich, Oktoberfest is also called *Wies'n*. This is a short version of *Theresienwiese*.

- Munich's Oktoberfest begins in September and ends on the first Sunday of October. The date of the celebration was moved to September because of October's chilly weather.

- German-American Day is celebrated throughout the United States on October 6. Like Oktoberfest, this special day honors German-American culture and history.

Words to Know

annual: every year

bodice: the part of a dress above the waist

emblems: signs that represent something

ethnic groups: groups of people that share a common culture, religion, or language

harvest: the gathering of crops

heritage: something handed down from parents to children

hinged: a joint on which a lid moves up and down

immigrated: moved away from one's homeland to begin life in a new country

polka: a lively dance that originated in Europe

waltzes: ballroom dances

yodeling: a type of singing

Index